I0002218

i

This is for everyone who has ever worried about their personal information online. This book is here to help you take control of your digital security.

Table of Content

Introduction: Why Cybersecurity Matters

The Growing Need for Online Security

The world today is more connected than ever. We shop online, communicate through emails and social media, store sensitive information in the cloud, and even handle financial transactions digitally. While this convenience has made our lives easier, it has also opened the door to numerous security risks. Cybercriminals, hackers, and fraudsters are constantly looking for ways to exploit vulnerabilities, steal data, and cause harm.

Every day, thousands of cyber-attacks occur across the globe, affecting individuals, businesses, and even governments. Identity theft, financial fraud, ransomware attacks, and data breaches are just a few of the threats that can disrupt lives and businesses. The rise of artificial intelligence, automation, and the Internet of Things (IoT) has only increased the complexity of online security, making it essential for everyone to be aware of the risks and take proactive steps to protect themselves.

But cybersecurity isn't just for IT professionals or big corporations—it's for everyone. Whether you're a student, a working professional, a business owner, or a retiree, your digital presence is at risk if you don't take cybersecurity seriously. In this book, we will explore the critical aspects of staying safe online, providing practical steps that anyone can follow to protect their personal information and secure their digital footprint.

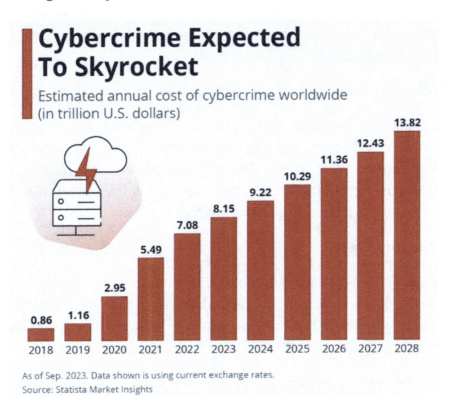

Cybercrime Expected To Skyrocket

Estimated annual cost of cybercrime worldwide (in trillion U.S. dollars)

Year	Value
2018	0.86
2019	1.16
2020	2.95
2021	5.49
2022	7.08
2023	8.15
2024	9.22
2025	10.29
2026	11.36
2027	12.43
2028	13.82

As of Sep. 2023. Data shown is using current exchange rates.
Source: Statista Market Insights

Understanding Cyber Threats: The Risks You Face

Cyber threats come in many forms, each with different consequences. Some can lead to financial loss, while others can compromise personal data, damage reputations, or even put physical safety at risk. Here are some of the most common cyber threats you should be aware of:

1. Malware Attacks

Malware, short for "malicious software," is a term used to describe harmful programs such as viruses, trojans, spyware, and ransomware. These programs can infect your computer or smartphone, steal your data, spy on your activities, or even lock you out of your files until a ransom is paid.

2. Phishing Scams

Phishing is a deceptive technique used by cybercriminals to trick individuals into revealing personal information such as passwords, credit card numbers, or social security numbers. These attacks often come in the form of fake emails, text messages, or fraudulent websites that appear to be from legitimate sources.

3. Identity Theft

Hackers can steal personal information and use it to commit fraud, take out loans, or gain unauthorized access to accounts. Once your identity is stolen, it can take years to fully recover from the damage caused.

4. Online Scams and Fraud

Fake job offers, investment scams, and fraudulent e-commerce websites are designed to trick unsuspecting victims into handing over their money or sensitive details. These scams are becoming increasingly sophisticated and difficult to detect.

5. Data Breaches

When companies or online services suffer security breaches, hackers can gain access to massive amounts of personal data. If your information is leaked, it can be used for fraud, blackmail, or other malicious activities.

Understanding these threats is the first step toward protecting yourself. Throughout this book, we will break down how these cyber threats work and what you can do to stay safe.

Who This Book is For and What You Will Learn

This book is designed for anyone who uses the internet, whether for personal or professional purposes. You don't need any prior technical knowledge to understand and implement the security measures discussed here. The goal is to provide simple, practical, and effective cybersecurity strategies that anyone can follow.

By the end of this book, you will learn:

- How to recognize and prevent cyber threats

- How to create strong passwords and protect your online accounts
- The importance of antivirus software and firewalls
- How to browse the internet safely and avoid scams
- How to protect your personal information and maintain privacy
- Safe online shopping and banking practices
- The role of cybersecurity in protecting children and families online
- Steps to take if you become a victim of a cyber attack

No matter your age, profession, or level of experience with technology, this book will help you become more cyber-aware and confident in navigating the digital world safely.

How to Use This Guide Effectively

To get the most out of this book, follow these guidelines:

1. Read Step by Step

Each chapter builds on the previous one, so it's best to follow the content in order. If you're completely new to cybersecurity, start from the beginning and gradually work your way through.

2. Apply What You Learn

Cybersecurity isn't just about reading—it's about action. After learning a new concept, take the necessary steps to secure your devices, update your passwords, or enable security features on your accounts.

3. Use the Checklists and Guides

Throughout this book, you'll find checklists, action plans, and step-by-step instructions. Use them to ensure that you're implementing best practices correctly.

4. Keep This Book as a Reference

Cybersecurity is an ongoing process, not a one-time task. Threats evolve, and new risks emerge, so revisit the book whenever you need a refresher or encounter a new security challenge.

5. Share with Friends and Family

Cybersecurity is not just an individual effort—it's a collective responsibility. Encourage your loved ones to adopt safe online habits and share key takeaways from this book with them.

By following these principles, you'll not only learn how to protect yourself from cyber threats but also gain the confidence to navigate the digital world securely. Now, let's dive in and start building your cybersecurity skills!

Chapter 1: Understanding Cyber Threats

The Different Types of Cyber Threats

Malware (Viruses, Trojans, Ransomware)

In the world of cybersecurity, one of the most common and dangerous threats you will encounter is **malware**. Malware, short for "malicious software," refers to any program or file designed to infiltrate, damage, or disrupt a system without the user's consent. Malware comes in various forms, each with its own purpose and level of damage.

1. Viruses

A virus is a malicious program that attaches itself to a legitimate file or program and spreads when the infected file is executed. Much like a biological virus, it requires a host and relies on human interaction to spread from one system to another. Viruses can delete files, corrupt data, or even take control of an entire system.

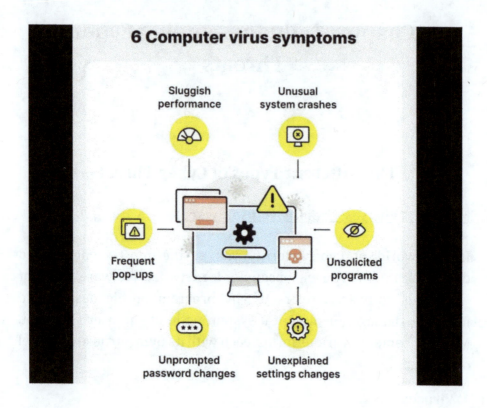

2. Trojans

Named after the infamous Trojan Horse, Trojans disguise themselves as legitimate software or files to deceive users into downloading and installing them. Unlike viruses, Trojans do not replicate themselves but create a backdoor for cybercriminals to access and control the infected system remotely.

3. Ransomware

Ransomware is one of the most dangerous types of malware. It encrypts a user's files and demands a ransom, usually in cryptocurrency, in exchange for the decryption key. If the ransom is not paid, the victim risks losing access to their files permanently.

How to Protect Yourself from Malware:

- Always use **trusted antivirus software** and keep it updated.
- Avoid downloading files or clicking on links from unknown sources.
- Regularly **update your operating system** to patch security vulnerabilities.
- Enable **firewalls** to prevent unauthorized access.

Phishing and Social Engineering Attacks

Cybercriminals have become highly skilled at **manipulating human psychology** to gain access to sensitive information. This is known as

social engineering, with phishing being one of the most common tactics used.

1. Phishing Attacks

Phishing is an attempt to trick individuals into revealing confidential information, such as login credentials, financial details, or personal data. These attacks typically occur via email, where a hacker impersonates a legitimate organization and urges the recipient to click on a malicious link or download an infected attachment.

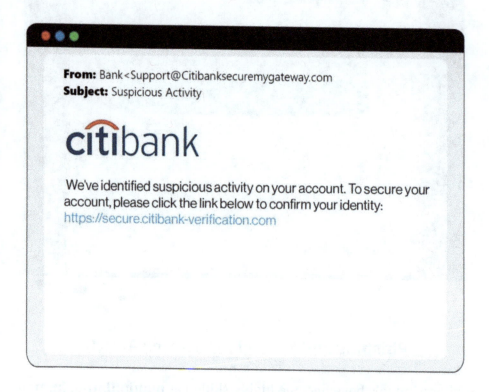

2. Spear Phishing

Spear phishing is a more targeted version of phishing. Attackers customize their messages for specific individuals or organizations by using personal details to make the attack more convincing.

3. Vishing and Smishing

- **Vishing** (voice phishing) occurs over phone calls, where attackers impersonate legitimate entities (such as banks or tech support) to steal information.
- **Smishing** (SMS phishing) involves sending fake text messages with malicious links or requests for sensitive data.

How to Avoid Phishing Attacks:

- Be cautious of **emails or messages urging immediate action**.
- Always **verify links** by hovering over them before clicking.
- Enable **two-factor authentication (2FA)** on accounts for added security.
- **Never share sensitive information** via email, phone, or text unless you are certain of the recipient's identity.

Identity Theft and Data Breaches

Identity theft occurs when cybercriminals steal your personal information—such as your name, Social Security number, or banking details—to commit fraud. **Data breaches** play a major role in identity theft, as massive amounts of personal data get exposed and sold on the dark web.

How Does Identity Theft Happen?

- **Phishing scams** trick users into revealing sensitive information.
- **Data breaches** expose personal and financial details stored by companies.
- **Malware infections** steal login credentials and credit card information.
- **Public Wi-Fi networks** allow hackers to intercept data from unsuspecting users.

How to Protect Yourself from Identity Theft:

- Use **strong and unique passwords** for every online account.
- **Monitor your financial statements** for any unauthorized transactions.
- Enable **fraud alerts** and **credit monitoring** services.
- **Avoid sharing personal details** on public forums and social media.

Online Scams and Fraud

The internet is filled with scams designed to steal your money, information, or both. Scammers use fake websites, fraudulent advertisements, and manipulative tactics to deceive victims.

Common Online Scams

- **Lottery and Sweepstakes Scams** – Fraudulent messages claiming you won a prize and need to pay a fee to claim it.

- **Tech Support Scams** – Fake calls or pop-ups warning you of computer issues and urging you to pay for unnecessary services.
- **Romance Scams** – Criminals create fake online dating profiles to gain victims' trust and ask for money.
- **Investment and Cryptocurrency Scams** – Promises of guaranteed high returns in exchange for upfront payments.

How to Avoid Online Scams:

- Always **verify sources** before providing any personal information.
- **Never send money** to someone you have only met online.

- Be skeptical of **unrealistic offers or urgent requests for action**.
- Use **reputable websites** for online transactions.

How Hackers Exploit Vulnerabilities

Hackers exploit weaknesses in systems to gain unauthorized access. These vulnerabilities can be due to outdated software, weak passwords, or misconfigured security settings.

<u>Common Vulnerabilities Exploited by Hackers:</u>

- **Unpatched Software** – Outdated programs contain security flaws that hackers exploit.
- **Weak Passwords** – Easily guessable passwords make it simple for hackers to gain access.
- **Open Ports and Unsecured Networks** – Hackers exploit unsecured network connections.
- **Human Error** – Mistakes like clicking on a malicious link can give hackers access.

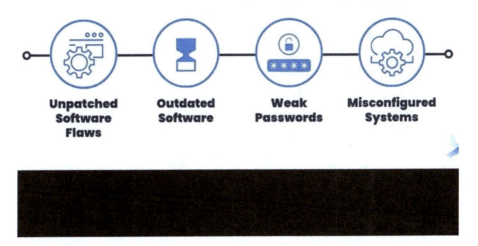

FOUR TYPES OF VULNERABILITIES

Unpatched Software Flaws — **Outdated Software** — **Weak Passwords** — **Misconfigured Systems**

How to Prevent Exploits:

- Keep **software and operating systems updated**.
- Use **complex passwords** and enable 2FA.
- Secure your **Wi-Fi network** with strong encryption.
- Train yourself to recognize **suspicious emails and websites**.

Recognizing Common Warning Signs of Cyber Threats

Understanding the early warning signs of cyber threats can help prevent damage before it happens.

17

1. Unusual Computer Behavior

- Slower performance
- Frequent crashes or freezing
- Unexpected pop-ups

2. Unauthorized Account Access

- Passwords no longer work
- Unrecognized login attempts
- Unusual account activity (e.g., emails sent from your account that you didn't write)

3. Suspicious Emails or Messages

- Emails urging immediate action
- Requests for sensitive information
- Links to unknown websites

What to Do If You Suspect a Cyber Threat:

- **Run a full system scan** with updated antivirus software.
- **Change compromised passwords immediately**.
- **Report suspicious activity** to the appropriate authorities.
- **Disconnect from the internet** to prevent further data leaks.

By staying aware and proactive, you can significantly reduce your risk of falling victim to cyber threats. The key to online safety is knowledge, awareness, and taking simple but effective precautions.

Chapter 2: Creating Strong Passwords and Securing Your Accounts

Why Weak Passwords Are a Huge Risk

Think of a password as the key to your digital home. If that key is too simple or easy to duplicate, it won't take much for an intruder to enter and take control. Many people still use passwords like "123456," "password," or even their own name, thinking that a hacker won't specifically target them. But the reality is, cybercriminals use automated tools to guess passwords at an alarming speed, and weak passwords make their job effortless.

A weak password poses several dangers:

- **Unauthorized Access:** If a hacker cracks your password, they can gain access to sensitive information, such as emails, banking details, and private conversations.
- **Identity Theft:** Once someone has access to your personal information, they can impersonate you, commit fraud, or access other accounts linked to your identity.
- **Financial Loss:** Many cybercriminals aim to steal credit card details or banking information, leading to direct financial losses.
- **Data Loss or Destruction:** Hackers can delete files, lock you out of accounts, or even demand ransom in exchange for access to your own data.

The best way to prevent these risks is to create strong, unique passwords for every account you use. Before we get into how to do that, let's understand how hackers attempt to crack passwords.

How Hackers Crack Passwords (and How to Stop Them)

Cybercriminals use several methods to crack passwords. Understanding these techniques can help you take steps to defend against them.

1. Brute-Force Attacks

This method involves systematically trying every possible password combination until the correct one is found. Automated tools can test millions of password variations within minutes. Short and simple passwords are the easiest to crack this way.

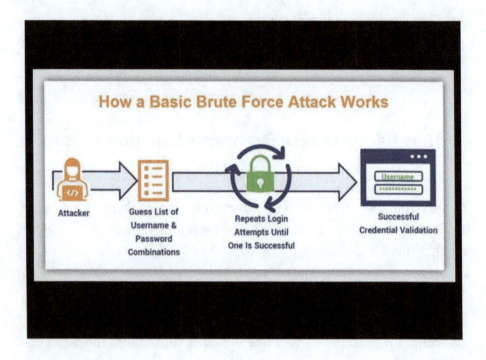

How to Stop It:

- Use long passwords (at least 12–16 characters).
- Avoid common words or predictable patterns.
- Use numbers, symbols, and uppercase/lowercase letters.

2. Dictionary Attacks

In a dictionary attack, hackers use a precompiled list of commonly used passwords and phrases to try and guess your password. This method is faster than a brute-force attack because it eliminates random guessing.

How to Stop It:

- Never use a single word from the dictionary as your password.

- Mix words with numbers and special characters to create an unpredictable combination.

3. Phishing Attacks

Hackers trick you into revealing your password by sending fake emails, messages, or website links that appear legitimate. These links often lead to counterfeit login pages that steal your credentials.

How to Stop It:

- Never click on suspicious links or emails.
- Always check the URL before entering your credentials.
- Enable two-factor authentication (2FA) for extra security.

4. Credential Stuffing

This happens when hackers obtain passwords from data breaches and try them on different accounts, assuming users reuse the same password across multiple sites.

How to Stop It:

- Use unique passwords for every account.
- Regularly update passwords, especially after a reported data breach.

Now that you understand the risks, let's go through the best practices for creating and managing strong passwords.

Creating and Managing Strong, Unique Passwords

A strong password is the first line of defense against cyber threats. But what makes a password strong? Here are some essential characteristics:

What Makes a Password Strong?

- **Length:** At least 12-16 characters long.
- **Complexity:** A mix of uppercase and lowercase letters, numbers, and special symbols.
- **Unpredictability:** Avoid using common words, phrases, or sequences (like "abc123" or "password1").
- **Uniqueness:** Do not reuse passwords for multiple accounts.

How to Create Strong Passwords

One of the easiest ways to create a strong password is by using a **passphrase**—a sequence of random words or a nonsensical sentence.

Example of a strong passphrase:
⊘ Bad: dog123
✓ Good: Purple-Tree#Jumps!Over9Clouds

You can also use a **password manager** to generate and store complex passwords for you.

The Role of Two-Factor Authentication (2FA)

Even a strong password isn't always enough. Two-factor authentication (2FA) adds an extra layer of security by requiring a second form of verification, such as:

- A one-time code sent to your phone.
- A fingerprint scan or face recognition.
- An authentication app (like Google Authenticator or Authy).

Why 2FA is Essential

Even if a hacker manages to steal your password, they won't be able to access your account without the second authentication factor. That's why enabling 2FA is one of the most effective ways to protect your online accounts.

How to Set Up 2FA

- **Go to your account's security settings.** Most major websites (Google, Facebook, banking apps) have an option for 2FA.
- **Choose your preferred 2FA method.** Common options include SMS verification, authenticator apps, or physical security keys.
- **Follow the setup instructions.** Usually, this involves scanning a QR code or entering a phone number.
- **Test your 2FA.** Log out and try logging back in to make sure 2FA is working correctly.

Secure Ways to Store and Protect Your Passwords

A strong password is useless if it's written down on a sticky note where anyone can see it. Here's how to store passwords securely:

1. Use a Password Manager

A password manager stores all your passwords in an encrypted vault, so you only need to remember **one master password**.

Popular password managers:

- Bitwarden
- LastPass
- 1Password
- Dashlane

2. Enable Auto-Generated Passwords

Many browsers and password managers offer a feature to generate random, complex passwords automatically. Always enable this option when creating new accounts.

3. Keep Your Master Password Secure

If you use a password manager, make sure your master password is:

- **Extremely strong** (use a passphrase, not a simple password).
- **Not stored anywhere visible** (avoid writing it down).
- **Memorized or stored in a secure location** (if written down, keep it in a locked safe).

4. Avoid Storing Passwords in Browsers

While browsers offer to save passwords, they are not as secure as dedicated password managers. Hackers can extract saved passwords from a compromised device.

5. Regularly Change Important Passwords

For highly sensitive accounts (email, banking, work-related platforms), change your password every few months, especially if there has been a security breach.

Final Thoughts

Your password security is your **first and strongest line of defense** against cyber threats. By using **strong, unique passwords**, enabling **two-factor authentication**, and securing your passwords properly, you significantly reduce the chances of being hacked. Take a moment now to update your passwords and enable 2FA wherever possible. Your future self will thank you!

Chapter 3: Protecting Your Devices (Computers, Phones, and Tablets)

In today's digital world, our devices—computers, smartphones, and tablets—hold a vast amount of personal, financial, and professional information. Without proper security measures, these devices become easy targets for hackers, malware, and cyber threats. Understanding how to protect them is crucial to maintaining your privacy and security. This chapter will guide you through essential steps to secure your devices effectively and ensure they remain safe from cyber threats.

The Importance of Keeping Your Operating System Updated

Your device's operating system (OS) is the backbone of its functionality, and keeping it updated is one of the simplest yet most effective ways to enhance security. Cybercriminals constantly look for vulnerabilities in outdated operating systems to exploit them, gaining access to personal information, files, and even financial data.

Why Updating Your OS is Crucial

- **Fixing Security Vulnerabilities** – Updates include security patches that close loopholes hackers use to infiltrate systems.
- **Improving Performance** – Updates often optimize system speed and fix bugs that slow down your device.
- **Enhancing Compatibility** – Many apps and software require the latest OS version to function smoothly.
- **Protecting Against New Threats** – Cyber threats evolve rapidly, and updates ensure your system stays prepared.

How to Keep Your OS Updated

- **For Windows:** Go to *Settings > Update & Security > Windows Update* and check for updates.

- **For macOS:** Click on *System Preferences > Software Update* and install the latest version.
- **For iOS & Android:** Navigate to *Settings > System Update* and check for available updates.

Enabling automatic updates ensures that your device remains protected without manual intervention.

Using Antivirus and Anti-Malware Software Effectively

Antivirus and anti-malware software act as the first line of defense against harmful software that could compromise your data and device functionality.

Understanding Antivirus vs. Anti-Malware

- **Antivirus software** primarily detects and removes traditional viruses, worms, and trojans.
- **Anti-malware software** targets modern threats like spyware, ransomware, and adware.

How to Use Security Software Effectively

- **Choose a Reliable Software** – Opt for reputable antivirus solutions such as Norton, McAfee, Bitdefender, or Windows Defender.
- **Keep Your Antivirus Updated** – Regular updates ensure your software recognizes the latest threats.

- **Schedule Regular Scans** – Set weekly or monthly scans to detect and remove potential threats before they cause harm.
- **Enable Real-Time Protection** – This feature continuously monitors your system for suspicious activity.
- **Avoid Free or Unverified Software** – Many free security programs are ineffective or even carry hidden malware.

Using a combination of antivirus and anti-malware tools can provide comprehensive protection for your device.

Setting Up Firewalls for Extra Protection

A firewall is a security system that monitors and controls incoming and outgoing network traffic, acting as a barrier between your device and potential cyber threats.

Why Firewalls Are Important

- **Blocks Unauthorized Access** – Prevents hackers from remotely accessing your computer.
- **Monitors Network Traffic** – Detects and stops suspicious connections.
- **Reduces Malware Infection Risks** – Helps prevent malicious software from communicating with external servers.

How to Enable a Firewall

- **Windows:** Go to *Control Panel > System and Security > Windows Defender Firewall* and ensure it's turned on.
- **macOS:** Navigate to *System Preferences > Security & Privacy > Firewall* and activate it.
- **Routers & Network Firewalls:** Most modern routers have built-in firewalls. Access your router's settings via its IP address and enable the firewall function.

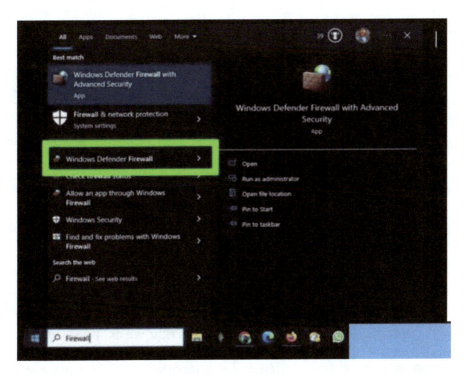

For added security, consider using third-party firewall software for more advanced control over network access.

How to Secure Your Smartphone and Prevent Unauthorized Access

Smartphones are a goldmine for cybercriminals due to the amount of personal and financial data they store. Securing your smartphone ensures that your data remains safe from unauthorized access.

Best Practices for Smartphone Security

- **Use a Strong Lock Screen Password** – Set a PIN, pattern, fingerprint, or facial recognition for security.
- **Enable Find My Device** – Activate *Find My iPhone* (iOS) or *Find My Device* (Android) to locate or remotely wipe lost phones.
- **Install Apps Only from Trusted Sources** – Avoid third-party app stores that may host malicious apps.
- **Review App Permissions** – Check what data each app can access and restrict unnecessary permissions.
- **Keep Your Software Updated** – Regular updates protect against security vulnerabilities.
- **Avoid Public Charging Stations** – Cybercriminals can use public USB ports to install malware (known as "juice jacking").

These measures ensure that your smartphone remains protected against common threats.

The Risks of Public Wi-Fi and How to Stay Safe

Public Wi-Fi networks, such as those in cafes, airports, or hotels, pose serious security risks as they are often unsecured and vulnerable to hackers.

Dangers of Public Wi-Fi

- **Man-in-the-Middle Attacks** – Hackers intercept data between your device and the network.

- **Malware Distribution** – Some networks can inject malware into connected devices.
- **Fake Hotspots** – Cybercriminals set up fake Wi-Fi networks to steal user credentials.

Risks of Public Wi-Fi Usage

How to Stay Safe on Public Wi-Fi

- **Avoid Accessing Sensitive Accounts** – Never log into banking apps or email on public networks.
- **Use a VPN (Virtual Private Network)** – Encrypts your internet connection, making it harder for hackers to steal data.

VPN Secure Connection

Get extra privacy anywhere you go online. VPN secures your internet connection to ensure your online activities can't be spied on.

Status | **Settings**

Automatically turn on VPN
We recommend using VPN during certain activities that require more privacy, like banking or shopping.

🛜 When connecting to untrusted networks
🏛 When banking
🛒 When shopping
👁 When accessing sensitive content
▶ When streaming
🔁 When torrenting

- **Turn Off Auto-Connect** – Disable automatic Wi-Fi connection on your device to prevent it from joining insecure networks.
- **Forget Networks After Use** – Remove public Wi-Fi networks from your saved connections list.
- **Use Mobile Data Instead** – If possible, use your phone's cellular network for better security.

By being cautious and following these best practices, you can minimize the risks associated with public Wi-Fi and keep your data secure.

Conclusion

Securing your devices is a crucial step in maintaining your online safety. By keeping your operating system updated, using antivirus software, setting up firewalls, securing your smartphone, and practicing safe browsing habits on public Wi-Fi, you significantly reduce the risk of cyber threats. Implement these security measures today to ensure your digital world remains protected against cybercriminals.

Chapter 4: Safe Internet Browsing Practices

Browsing the internet is an essential part of our daily lives, but it comes with risks. Cybercriminals create deceptive websites, track your online activities, and attempt to steal sensitive information. Understanding safe browsing practices is crucial for protecting your personal data and ensuring a secure online experience. This chapter will guide you through key concepts and step-by-step methods to enhance your online safety.

How to Identify and Avoid Phishing Websites

What is a Phishing Website?

Phishing websites are fraudulent sites designed to look like legitimate ones, tricking users into entering personal details such as usernames, passwords, or credit card numbers. Cybercriminals often send phishing emails with links to these fake sites, making them appear as if they are from trusted organizations like banks, social media platforms, or online retailers.

How Phishing Websites Work

- **Impersonation of Legitimate Websites** – The attackers create a nearly identical copy of a trusted website.

- **Use of Urgent or Scary Messages** – Phishing emails often claim that your account has been compromised or that immediate action is needed.
- **Tricking Users into Entering Credentials** – When you enter your login details, the attackers capture them and gain access to your real account.

Signs of a Phishing Website

- **Suspicious URL** – Hover over the link before clicking. Fake websites often have slight misspellings (e.g., amaz0n.com instead of amazon.com).
- **No HTTPS Security** – If the website lacks HTTPS (a padlock icon in the address bar), it may not be secure.
- **Poor Design or Grammar Errors** – Legitimate companies rarely have typos or poorly designed pages.
- **Unexpected Pop-Ups** – Phishing sites often use pop-ups that ask for sensitive information.
- **Unusual Requests for Personal Information** – Banks and reputable companies will never ask for passwords or Social Security numbers via email.

Steps to Avoid Phishing Websites

- **Do Not Click on Suspicious Links** – Always manually type the website address instead of clicking on links from emails.
- **Verify Website Authenticity** – Check the official website before entering login details.
- **Use Browser Security Features** – Most modern browsers warn users when visiting unsafe websites.

- **Enable Multi-Factor Authentication (MFA)** – Even if credentials are stolen, MFA adds an extra layer of security.
- **Report Suspicious Websites** – If you suspect a site is phishing, report it to your browser or cybersecurity authorities.

The Importance of HTTPS and Secure Connections

What is HTTPS?

HTTPS (HyperText Transfer Protocol Secure) ensures that data sent between your browser and a website is encrypted, making it difficult for hackers to intercept.

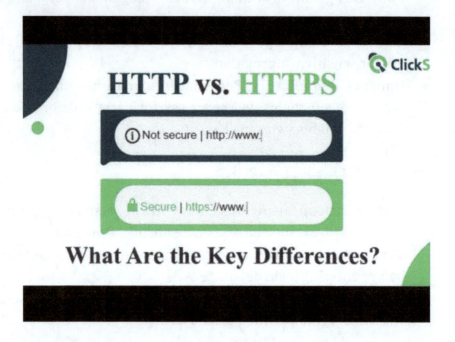

Why HTTPS is Important

- **Encryption** – Protects your login credentials, payment information, and private messages.
- **Authentication** – Confirms that the website is legitimate and not a phishing site.
- **Data Integrity** – Prevents unauthorized modifications to web content.

How to Ensure Secure Connections

- **Always Look for the Padlock Icon** – Ensure a website has a secure connection before entering sensitive data.
- **Avoid Entering Information on HTTP Websites** – If a site does not use HTTPS, do not enter personal details.
- **Use a Secure Browser Extension** – Many browser add-ons force HTTPS connections for better security.
- **Verify Certificates** – Click on the padlock icon to check the SSL certificate details.
- **Be Wary of Fake HTTPS Sites** – Some phishing sites may use HTTPS but still be fraudulent. Always verify the domain name.

Using Private Browsing, VPNs, and Proxy Servers

Private Browsing Mode

Private browsing, also known as "Incognito Mode," prevents your browser from storing your search history, cookies, and form data.

When to Use Private Browsing

- Prevent tracking on shared computers.
- Avoid storing sensitive login credentials.
- Research sensitive topics without leaving a history trail.

VPNs (Virtual Private Networks)

A VPN encrypts your internet traffic and routes it through a secure server, hiding your IP address and preventing third parties from tracking your online activity.

Benefits of Using a VPN

- Enhanced privacy by masking your IP address.
- Protection when using public Wi-Fi.

- Access to geo-restricted content securely.

How to Choose a Good VPN

- **Look for Strong Encryption** – AES-256 encryption is highly secure.
- **No-Logs Policy** – Ensure the provider does not store your browsing data.
- **Fast Connection Speeds** – Slow VPNs can make browsing frustrating.
- **Compatible with Your Devices** – Check if it works on all platforms you use.

Proxy Servers

A proxy server acts as an intermediary between your computer and the internet, hiding your IP address and filtering content.

When to Use a Proxy Server

- Bypassing geo-restrictions.
- Enhancing online privacy without using a VPN.
- Blocking malicious sites in a controlled network.

Managing Cookies and Preventing Online Tracking

What Are Cookies?

Cookies are small files stored on your device by websites to remember preferences, login details, and browsing behavior.

How Websites Track You

- **Third-Party Cookies** – Advertisers track your behavior across multiple sites.
- **Fingerprinting** – Websites collect device and browser information to identify users.
- **Tracking Scripts** – Code that follows your activities and collects data.

How to Reduce Online Tracking

- **Block Third-Party Cookies** – Adjust browser settings to prevent cross-site tracking.
- **Use Privacy-Focused Browsers** – Some browsers like Brave and Firefox offer built-in tracking protection.
- **Enable Do Not Track (DNT)** – Though not enforced by all websites, it signals sites not to track your activity.
- **Use Anti-Tracking Browser Extensions** – Tools like uBlock Origin and Privacy Badger help block tracking scripts.

Recognizing and Avoiding Dangerous Pop-Ups and Ads

Why Pop-Ups and Ads Can Be Dangerous

Many malicious websites use pop-ups and ads to distribute malware, trick users into downloading harmful software, or redirect them to phishing sites.

How to Identify Harmful Pop-Ups

- **Unexpected Warnings** – Messages claiming your computer is infected.
- **Fake Close Buttons** – Some pop-ups trigger downloads even when clicked.
- **Redirects to Unfamiliar Sites** – Clicking ads may take you to sketchy websites.

How to Avoid Pop-Up and Ad Threats

- **Use a Reliable Ad Blocker** – Browser extensions like AdBlock or uBlock Origin can prevent harmful ads.
- **Disable Pop-Ups in Your Browser** – Adjust browser settings to block pop-ups automatically.
- **Never Click on Suspicious Ads** – Avoid clicking on ads offering free software downloads or prizes.
- **Close Pop-Ups Safely** – If a pop-up appears, close it using the browser's built-in exit button rather than interacting with it.

Chapter 5: Email and Social Media Security

The internet is a powerful tool for communication, networking, and sharing experiences, but it also presents risks that can threaten your privacy and security. Among the most vulnerable areas are **email and social media accounts**, which are often targeted by hackers, scammers, and malicious entities. Understanding how to **recognize and prevent cyber threats** in these areas is essential to safeguarding your personal information.

In this chapter, we will explore how to detect fake emails and phishing attempts, secure your social media accounts, adjust privacy settings, and avoid the risks of oversharing personal information. We will also cover what to do if your email or social media account gets hacked.

Recognizing Fake Emails and Phishing Attempts

Phishing is one of the most common and effective cyberattacks. It occurs when a scammer **impersonates a legitimate entity** to trick you into providing sensitive information such as passwords, bank details, or personal data. These attacks often happen through fake emails, messages, or links that appear trustworthy but are actually designed to steal your credentials.

How to Identify a Phishing Email

Phishing emails often have certain red flags that distinguish them from legitimate messages. Here are some key signs to watch out for:

- **Suspicious Sender Address** – The email might claim to be from a trusted source, but if you closely inspect the sender's address, you may notice **misspellings** or **random numbers/letters** in the domain.

  Example: Instead of support@paypal.com, a phishing email might come from support@pay-pal.info.

- **Generic Greetings** – Legitimate organizations typically use your name in communications, while phishing emails often use vague greetings like "Dear User" or "Dear Customer."

- **Urgent or Threatening Language** – Scammers create a sense of urgency to make you act quickly, such as:
  - "Your account will be suspended if you do not verify it immediately."
  - "We've detected unauthorized activity. Log in now to secure your account."

- **Unexpected Attachments or Links** – Phishing emails often contain links to fraudulent websites or attachments that install malware. Before clicking, **hover over the link** to check if it directs you to a legitimate website.

  Example: Instead of https://www.bankofamerica.com, a phishing link may appear as https://www.bankofamerica.secure-login.xyz.

- **Poor Grammar and Formatting** – Many phishing emails contain **spelling mistakes, awkward phrasing, and**

improper punctuation, which are rare in official communications.

How to Protect Yourself from Phishing

- **Do not click on suspicious links** – Always visit official websites directly by typing the URL in your browser instead of clicking on email links.
- **Verify with the organization** – If you receive a suspicious email from a company, call their official support line or visit their website instead of replying.
- **Use email filtering tools** – Enable spam filters on your email provider to reduce the chances of phishing emails reaching your inbox.
- **Enable multi-factor authentication (MFA)** – Even if hackers steal your password, MFA adds an extra layer of security to prevent unauthorized access.

How to Safeguard Your Social Media Accounts

Social media platforms hold a vast amount of personal information, making them attractive targets for cybercriminals. If your account is compromised, attackers can impersonate you, steal private data, or even scam your friends and family.

Essential Security Steps for Social Media Accounts

- **Use Strong and Unique Passwords** – Do not reuse passwords across multiple platforms. Use a **password manager** to generate and store complex passwords.

- **Enable Two-Factor Authentication (2FA)** – This adds an extra layer of security by requiring a second verification step, such as a code sent to your phone or email.
- **Review Login Activity Regularly** – Most social media platforms allow you to check where and when your account was accessed. If you see an unfamiliar location or device, **log out of all devices** and change your password immediately.
- **Be Wary of Third-Party Apps** – Avoid granting unnecessary permissions to third-party apps that request access to your account.
- **Log Out on Shared or Public Devices** – If you use a public computer or someone else's phone, make sure to log out and clear browser data after use.

Adjusting Privacy Settings on Popular Platforms

Each social media platform offers privacy settings to help control who can see your information. Regularly reviewing and updating these settings minimizes your exposure to risks.

Facebook

- Set your profile to **private** so only friends can see your posts.
- Limit who can send you friend requests and messages.
- Enable **login alerts** to receive notifications of unrecognized logins.

Instagram

- Make your account **private** to restrict who can view your content.
- Turn off **activity status** so others can't see when you're online.
- Enable **two-factor authentication** for added security.

Twitter (X)

- Protect your tweets so only approved followers can see them.
- Disable **location sharing** in tweets.
- Restrict direct messages from unknown users.

The Dangers of Sharing Too Much Personal Information Online

Oversharing personal details on social media can expose you to identity theft, fraud, and cyberstalking. Common mistakes include:

- **Posting travel plans in real-time** – This signals when your home is empty and vulnerable to burglaries.
- **Sharing your full birthdate** – Birthdays are often used in security verification questions.
- **Posting personal contact information** – Scammers can use your phone number or email to launch phishing attacks.

How to Stay Safe

- Avoid posting sensitive details such as addresses, phone numbers, or financial data.
- Be cautious with **location tags and check-ins**.
- Think before you post – once something is online, it's hard to remove completely.

What to Do If Your Email or Social Media Account Gets Hacked

If you suspect your account has been compromised, act quickly to minimize damage.

Immediate Actions to Take

- **Change Your Password** – Use a strong, unique password and enable 2FA.
- **Log Out of All Sessions** – Most platforms allow you to remotely log out of all devices.
- **Check for Unauthorized Changes** – Review your account settings to see if any recovery emails or phone numbers were changed.
- **Warn Your Contacts** – Hackers often use compromised accounts to scam friends and family.
- **Report the Hack** – Contact the platform's support team to recover your account.
- **Scan Your Device for Malware** – If your credentials were stolen, malware might be involved.

Final Thoughts

Securing your email and social media accounts requires a proactive approach. By staying alert, using strong security measures, and adjusting your privacy settings, you can **significantly reduce the risk of cyber threats**. Make a habit of reviewing your accounts regularly, and always think before clicking on suspicious links or sharing personal details online.

By following these best practices, you'll not only protect yourself but also help create a safer digital environment for everyone.

Chapter 6: Safe Online Shopping and Banking

Online shopping and banking have made life more convenient, allowing us to buy products, pay bills, and manage our finances from the comfort of our homes. However, with this convenience comes the risk of fraud, scams, and data breaches. Understanding how to identify secure websites, use safe payment methods, and protect your financial information is crucial to staying safe in the digital world.

This chapter will guide you through essential practices to ensure your online transactions are secure. You will learn how to recognize legitimate e-commerce websites, use secure payment methods, protect your bank account, detect scams, and respond effectively if your financial information is compromised.

Identifying Trustworthy E-Commerce Websites

When shopping online, it is essential to ensure that the website you are using is legitimate and secure. Cybercriminals often create fake online stores that look genuine but are designed to steal personal and financial information. Here's how to identify a trustworthy e-commerce site:

Check for HTTPS and Secure Connections

A secure website will always use HTTPS (Hypertext Transfer Protocol Secure), which ensures that the data exchanged between you and the website is encrypted. Look for a padlock symbol in the browser's address bar. If a site only uses HTTP, avoid entering any personal information.

Verify the Website's Authenticity

- **Look for Contact Information**: A legitimate online store will have a physical address, phone number, and customer support email. If these details are missing or seem suspicious, it could be a fake website.
- **Check for Online Reviews**: Search for customer reviews and ratings on independent review sites such as Trustpilot, Better Business Bureau (BBB), or Google Reviews. Be cautious of websites with no reviews or overwhelmingly positive reviews that seem fake.
- **Look for Spelling and Grammar Mistakes**: Many fraudulent websites have poorly written content, spelling mistakes, and low-quality images. Professional businesses invest in well-designed websites.
- **Be Cautious of Too-Good-To-Be-True Deals**: If a product's price is significantly lower than on other websites, it might be a scam. Fraudsters use low prices to lure customers into providing their payment details.

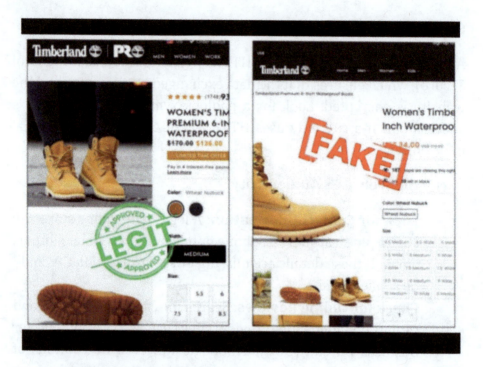

Avoid Clicking on Unverified Links

Many scammers use phishing emails and fake advertisements to trick users into visiting fraudulent e-commerce sites. Instead of clicking links from emails or social media, type the store's web address directly into your browser.

Secure Payment Methods and Avoiding Credit Card Fraud

Using the right payment methods can protect you from fraud and unauthorized transactions. Some payment options offer better security than others.

Preferred Payment Methods for Safety

- **Credit Cards**: Credit cards provide better fraud protection than debit cards. Most credit card companies offer chargeback services if you fall victim to fraud.
- **PayPal, Apple Pay, and Google Pay**: These digital wallets add an extra layer of security by keeping your payment details private.
- **Virtual Credit Cards**: Some banks offer virtual credit cards, which generate a temporary card number for one-time use, reducing the risk of fraud.
- **Avoid Direct Bank Transfers**: Scammers often ask for direct wire transfers or cryptocurrency payments because they are difficult to trace and reverse.

How to Protect Your Credit Card Information

- **Never Save Your Card Details on Websites**: If a website gets hacked, stored payment details can be stolen.
- **Use Two-Factor Authentication (2FA)**: Enable 2FA on your bank or credit card account to add an extra layer of security.
- **Monitor Your Transactions Regularly**: Check your bank statements frequently for any unauthorized charges and report them immediately.

Protecting Your Bank Account and Financial Information

Cybercriminals often target online banking users to steal sensitive financial data. To safeguard your bank account, follow these best practices:

Enable Strong Authentication

- Use multi-factor authentication (MFA) whenever possible.
- Set up alerts to notify you of any unusual account activity.

Secure Your Banking Devices

- Keep your smartphone and computer updated with the latest security patches.
- Install antivirus software to detect malicious activities.

Use Secure Networks

- Avoid accessing your bank account on public Wi-Fi. If necessary, use a VPN (Virtual Private Network) for added security.

Recognizing Phishing Attempts

- Banks will never ask for sensitive information via email or text. If you receive a suspicious message, contact your bank directly.
- Look out for fake banking websites designed to steal login credentials.

How to Detect and Avoid Online Shopping Scams

Online shopping scams come in various forms, but they often share common red flags. Understanding these can help you avoid falling victim.

Common Online Shopping Scams

- **Fake Stores**: Fraudsters create websites that mimic real online stores but never deliver the purchased items.
- **Non-Delivery Scams**: A seller receives payment but does not send the product.
- **Counterfeit Products**: Some sellers advertise branded products at extremely low prices but deliver cheap knockoffs.
- **Overpayment Scams**: Scammers send you a check for more than the purchase amount and ask you to refund the difference before their fake check bounces.

How to Avoid Online Scams

- Research unfamiliar online stores before purchasing.
- Only shop on well-known and reputable platforms like Amazon, Walmart, and major brand websites.
- If possible, use buyer protection services like PayPal's Purchase Protection.

Steps to Take If Your Financial Information is Compromised

Despite taking precautions, cybercriminals may still find ways to access your financial information. If you suspect fraud, take immediate action:

1. Contact Your Bank or Card Issuer

- Report unauthorized transactions immediately.
- Request to freeze or replace compromised cards.
- Enable fraud alerts to receive notifications about suspicious activity.

2. Change Your Passwords

- Update passwords for online banking, payment apps, and shopping accounts.
- Use a strong, unique password for each account.

3. Monitor Your Accounts Closely

- Review your recent transactions for unauthorized purchases.
- Check for any changes to your personal details in bank accounts and payment apps.

4. Report the Incident

- Report fraud to your bank, credit bureau, and local authorities.
- If you were scammed on an online marketplace, notify the platform (e.g., eBay, Amazon).

5. Place a Fraud Alert on Your Credit Report

- Contact credit reporting agencies to add a fraud alert, preventing identity thieves from opening new accounts in your name.

Final Thoughts

Online shopping and banking are essential parts of modern life, but they come with risks. By following the guidelines in this chapter, you can minimize the chances of becoming a victim of fraud and cybercrime. Always be cautious, verify the authenticity of websites, use secure payment methods, and monitor your financial accounts regularly. If you ever suspect fraud, act quickly to protect your financial security.

Chapter 7: Protecting Personal Data and Online Privacy

The internet is a powerful tool that connects us to information, people, and services across the world. However, every time we go online, we leave behind traces of personal information—some of which can be exploited by hackers, advertisers, and even legitimate businesses. Protecting your personal data is essential to maintaining online privacy and preventing unauthorized access to your sensitive information. In this chapter, we will discuss the types of information you should never share online, how advertisers and companies track you, managing privacy settings, understanding data breaches, and why regularly deleting unused accounts is important.

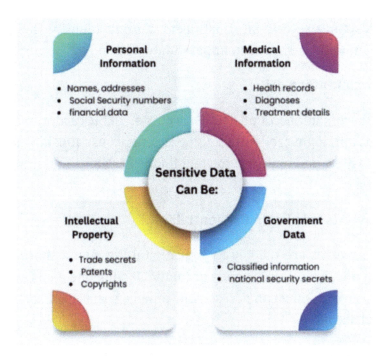

What Kind of Information You Should Never Share Online

Many people unknowingly expose personal details online without realizing the risks involved. The information you share on websites, social media, and other digital platforms can be used for identity theft, fraud, and other malicious activities. Here are some key types of information that should always be kept private:

1. Personal Identification Details

This includes your full name, home address, phone number, date of birth, and government-issued identification numbers (such as Social Security Number, Passport Number, or Driver's License Number).

Criminals can use this information to commit identity theft, open fraudulent accounts, or even impersonate you online.

2. Financial Information

Never share bank account details, credit or debit card numbers, or payment app login credentials. Cybercriminals use phishing attacks, fake websites, and malware to steal financial details and drain bank accounts.

3. Passwords and Login Credentials

Your passwords are the key to your digital life. Avoid sharing them with anyone, even close friends or family. If someone gains access to your password, they can access your emails, social media, and even financial accounts.

4. Work-Related or Confidential Information

Sensitive workplace information, company financials, or client data should never be shared online unless authorized. Leaking such data can lead to legal consequences and security risks for your employer.

5. Location Data

Posting your real-time location on social media or public forums can make you an easy target for criminals. Be cautious about sharing vacation plans, daily routines, or GPS-tagged photos that reveal where you are.

6. Private Conversations and Personal Messages

Anything shared in private chats, emails, or direct messages can be screenshotted, leaked, or hacked. Avoid discussing highly sensitive matters over unsecured digital platforms.

By keeping this information private, you reduce the risk of identity theft, financial fraud, and online harassment.

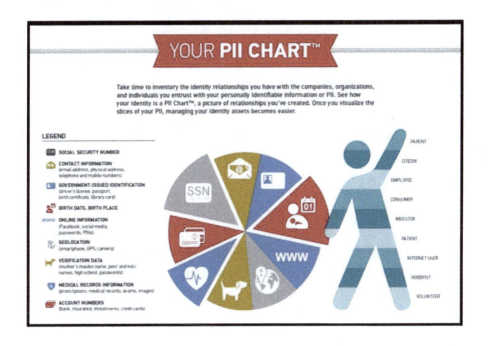

How Advertisers and Companies Track You Online

While cybercriminals pose a significant threat, companies and advertisers also collect vast amounts of data about users. This data is used for targeted advertising, analytics, and business growth. Here's how they track you:

1. Cookies and Tracking Pixels

Websites use cookies—small files stored on your browser—to remember your preferences, track browsing habits, and target you with personalized ads. Some cookies are necessary for websites to function, while others are used to track your activities across different sites.

2. Browser Fingerprinting

Even if you clear cookies, companies can still identify you using browser fingerprinting. This method collects information about your device, operating system, screen resolution, and installed fonts to create a unique profile.

3. Social Media and Account Logins

When you log in to websites using social media accounts (like Facebook or Google), those platforms can track your activity and gather data on your browsing habits. This allows advertisers to tailor ads based on your interests.

4. Mobile Apps and Permissions

Many smartphone apps request access to contacts, location, microphone, and camera—sometimes unnecessarily. If an app doesn't need certain permissions to function, deny access to prevent data collection.

5. Search Engines and Online Activity

Search engines like Google track your queries to provide better search results and deliver personalized advertisements. Even when using private browsing mode, search engines still collect data unless you take additional privacy measures.

Managing Privacy Settings on Websites and Apps

One of the best ways to protect your personal data is to adjust privacy settings on websites, apps, and devices. Here's how you can take control:

1. Review and Adjust Social Media Privacy Settings

- Set your profiles to private so only approved friends or followers can see your posts.
- Disable location tracking and tagging features.
- Limit who can send you friend requests or messages.
- Turn off data sharing with third-party apps.

2. Configure Web Browser Privacy Settings

- Use privacy-focused browsers like Brave or Firefox with enhanced tracking protection.
- Disable third-party cookies and install browser extensions like Privacy Badger.
- Enable "Do Not Track" settings (though not all websites honor this request).

3. Adjust Mobile App Permissions

- Review and disable unnecessary app permissions, such as microphone and location access.
- Delete apps you no longer use to prevent background data collection.

4. Opt Out of Targeted Advertising

- Many companies allow users to opt out of personalized ads through their account settings.

- Use services like the Digital Advertising Alliance (DAA) to manage advertising preferences.

Understanding Data Breaches and How They Affect You

A data breach occurs when hackers gain unauthorized access to sensitive data stored by companies, government agencies, or online services. This stolen information can be sold on the dark web, leading to identity theft, fraud, and blackmail.

How to Protect Yourself from Data Breaches

- Use unique passwords for each online account to minimize risks if one site is compromised.
- Enable two-factor authentication (2FA) to add an extra layer of security.
- Regularly monitor your bank statements and credit reports for suspicious activity.
- Sign up for breach notification services like Have I Been Pwned to get alerts if your data has been exposed.

The Importance of Regularly Deleting Unused Accounts

Old and unused accounts are often forgotten, but they still store valuable personal information that hackers can exploit. Regularly reviewing and deleting inactive accounts is a crucial step in protecting your digital identity.

Why Deleting Unused Accounts is Important

- Unused accounts may have weak or outdated security, making them an easy target for hackers.
- Companies may continue collecting and selling your data even if you no longer use their services.
- Breached inactive accounts can lead to unauthorized access to other linked services.

How to Find and Delete Old Accounts

- Check email inboxes for sign-up confirmation emails and newsletters from services you no longer use.
- Visit the website's settings page to find the account deletion option.
- If no deletion option exists, contact customer support and request account closure.
- Remove linked third-party accounts (e.g., Google or Facebook logins).

By managing and deleting old accounts, you can significantly reduce your online footprint and minimize security risks.

Conclusion

Protecting personal data and online privacy requires continuous effort. By being mindful of the information you share, understanding how companies track you, managing privacy settings, staying aware of data breaches, and deleting unused accounts, you take control of your digital presence. These proactive steps will help you stay safer online and keep your private information secure.

Chapter 8: Cybersecurity for Families and Children

The internet has become an essential part of everyday life, offering endless opportunities for learning, communication, and entertainment. However, it also comes with risks, especially for children and families who may not fully understand how to navigate the digital world safely. Cybersecurity for families is not just about installing security software; it's about educating children, setting boundaries, and creating a secure online environment. This chapter will help you understand how to protect your family from online threats while teaching children about digital responsibility.

Teaching Kids About Online Safety and Digital Responsibility

Children today grow up surrounded by technology. From an early age, they use smartphones, tablets, and computers to play games, watch videos, and communicate with friends. While technology is a fantastic tool, children must learn how to use it responsibly and safely.

Why Digital Responsibility Matters

Digital responsibility means understanding the impact of online actions. Everything shared online can be permanent, and careless behavior can lead to serious consequences. Teaching children about their digital footprint helps them think before they post, share, or click.

Key Online Safety Rules for Children

- **Never share personal information online** – Children should avoid posting their full name, address, school name, or phone number on the internet.
- **Use strong passwords** – Teach children to create strong passwords and never share them with anyone except parents.
- **Think before clicking links** – Not all websites are safe. Encourage children to ask a parent before clicking on unfamiliar links.
- **Be careful when talking to strangers online** – Online friends may not always be who they say they are. Children should never meet an online friend in person without parental supervision.
- **Report anything suspicious** – Encourage children to talk to a trusted adult if they encounter something inappropriate or feel uncomfortable online.
- **Limit screen time** – Excessive time online can lead to addiction and exposure to harmful content. Set boundaries for daily internet use.

Making Online Safety Fun and Engaging

Children learn best when they are engaged. Consider using games, quizzes, and storytelling to teach them about cybersecurity. Many educational websites offer interactive tools that make learning about online safety enjoyable.

Setting Up Parental Controls on Devices and Apps

Parental controls help protect children by restricting inappropriate content, managing screen time, and monitoring online activity. Most devices, apps, and internet service providers offer built-in parental control features.

How to Set Up Parental Controls

1. On Smartphones and Tablets

Apple Devices (iPhone/iPad)

- Go to **Settings** > **Screen Time**
- Enable **Content & Privacy Restrictions**
- Set limits on apps, web browsing, and purchases

Android Devices

- Open **Google Family Link**
- Create a child's account and set restrictions
- Block inappropriate apps and set screen time limits

2. On Web Browsers

Google Chrome: Enable **SafeSearch** in settings to filter explicit content.

Microsoft Edge: Use **Family Safety** settings to block harmful sites.

3. On Streaming Services (YouTube, Netflix, etc.)

Set up **YouTube Kids** for safer video content.

Use Netflix's **kid-friendly profile** feature.

Regularly Reviewing Settings

Parental controls are only effective if regularly updated. Check settings periodically to ensure they align with your child's age and online activities.

Recognizing and Preventing Cyberbullying

Cyberbullying is one of the biggest online dangers for children. It involves using digital platforms to harass, intimidate, or embarrass someone.

Signs Your Child Might Be a Victim of Cyberbullying

- Sudden withdrawal from social media or online activities
- Unexplained sadness, anxiety, or irritability
- Avoiding school or social interactions
- Hiding screens or devices when parents are nearby

How to Prevent Cyberbullying

- **Encourage Open Communication** – Let children know they can talk to you about anything that happens online.
- **Monitor Online Activity** – Keep an eye on social media interactions and messaging apps.
- **Set Privacy Controls** – Ensure children's accounts are private and only accessible to friends and family.
- **Teach Respectful Behavior** – Children should understand the impact of their words and actions online.
- **Report and Block Bullies** – Most platforms allow users to report inappropriate behavior and block harmful contacts.

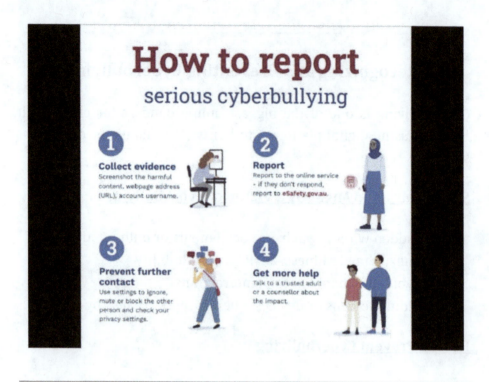

How to report
serious cyberbullying

1 Collect evidence
Screenshot the harmful content, webpage address (URL), account username.

2 Report
Report to the online service - if they don't respond, report to eSafety.gov.au.

3 Prevent further contact
Use settings to ignore, mute or block the other person and check your privacy settings.

4 Get more help
Talk to a trusted adult or a counsellor about the impact.

Keeping Your Family's Smart Devices and Home Network Secure

Your home network is the gateway to all internet-connected devices in your household. If it's not secure, hackers can gain access to personal information.

Steps to Secure Your Home Network

- **Change Default Router Passwords** – Many routers come with weak default passwords. Create a strong, unique password.

- **Enable WPA3 or WPA2 Encryption** – This protects your Wi-Fi network from unauthorized access.
- **Keep Software and Firmware Updated** – Regular updates fix security vulnerabilities.
- **Disable Remote Access** – This prevents hackers from controlling your router remotely.
- **Set Up a Guest Network** – Keep family devices on a private network and allow guests limited access.

Protecting Smart Devices (IoT Security)

Smart home devices like baby monitors, voice assistants, and cameras can be hacked if not properly secured.

- Always change factory passwords.
- Disable unnecessary features like remote access.
- Keep software updated to prevent security flaws.

Best Practices for Monitoring and Guiding Children's Internet Usage

Keeping children safe online requires active monitoring and guidance. However, it's important to balance supervision with respect for their privacy as they grow older.

How to Monitor Without Invading Privacy

- **Use Parental Control Software** – Tools like Qustodio or Norton Family provide insights without excessive spying.

- **Keep Screens Visible** – Place computers in shared spaces rather than private bedrooms.
- **Check Browsing History Together** – This helps educate children on appropriate content.
- **Encourage Honest Conversations** – Instead of secretive monitoring, discuss potential online dangers openly.
- **Establish Internet-Free Zones** – For example, no phones at the dinner table or before bedtime.

Building Healthy Digital Habits

- **Set Time Limits** – Avoid excessive screen time to promote healthy habits.
- **Encourage Offline Activities** – Engage children in outdoor play, reading, and family activities.
- **Be a Role Model** – Children learn by observing. Practice responsible screen use yourself.

Conclusion

Cybersecurity for families and children requires a combination of education, protective measures, and open communication. By teaching digital responsibility, setting up controls, and maintaining an active role in your child's online life, you can create a safe and positive internet experience for your family.

Chapter 9: Responding to Cybersecurity Threats

What to Do If You Suspect Your Computer or Phone is Infected

Understanding the Signs of Infection

The first step in handling a potential malware or virus infection is recognizing the symptoms. Modern malware can be highly sophisticated, often hiding in the background while stealing data or causing system disruptions. Here are common signs that your device may be infected:

- **Unexpected Pop-ups** – If you start seeing intrusive advertisements or messages that warn about an infection and prompt you to install software, it's a red flag.
- **Slow Performance** – A sudden drop in speed, frequent freezing, or applications crashing unexpectedly might indicate malware running in the background.
- **Unusual Battery Drain** – If your phone's battery drains quickly despite normal usage, it could be due to malicious applications running without your knowledge.
- **Unauthorized Changes to Settings** – Malware may alter system settings, disable security programs, or add new programs without your permission.
- **Unfamiliar Apps or Files** – If you notice programs or files you didn't download, it could indicate a security breach.

Immediate Steps to Contain the Threat

If you suspect your computer or phone is infected, take the following actions immediately:

- **Disconnect from the Internet** – This prevents the malware from communicating with its source or spreading to other devices.
- **Reboot into Safe Mode** – Restarting your computer in safe mode prevents malware from running automatically. On mobile devices, use Safe Mode to troubleshoot suspicious apps.
- **Run a Full Security Scan** – Use a reputable antivirus or anti-malware program to detect and remove threats.
- **Uninstall Suspicious Programs or Apps** – Remove any applications you do not recognize or that were installed without your consent.
- **Update Your Software** – Ensure your operating system and all applications are up to date to patch security vulnerabilities.
- **Change Your Passwords** – If you suspect keylogging malware, update your passwords after confirming the infection has been removed.
- **Backup Important Files** – Save important data to an external drive or secure cloud storage in case a factory reset is required.

If the issue persists, consider seeking professional assistance or performing a full factory reset on your device.

Steps to Take If Your Account is Hacked

Recognizing a Compromised Account

A hacked account can be identified through warning signs such as:

- Unauthorized transactions or activity
- Password reset emails you didn't request
- Friends receiving spam messages from your account
- Inability to access your account

Immediate Actions to Recover Your Account

If you suspect that one of your online accounts has been compromised, follow these steps to regain control:

- **Attempt to Reset Your Password** – Use the 'Forgot Password' option to regain access. Ensure the new password is strong and unique.
- **Check Associated Email and Phone Number** – Verify that the account's recovery email and phone number have not been changed.
- **Enable Two-Factor Authentication (2FA)** – If 2FA is not enabled, activate it immediately to add an extra layer of security.
- **Review Account Activity** – Check login history for unfamiliar locations or devices.
- **Notify Your Contacts** – Alert friends and family to avoid clicking on malicious links sent from your account.
- **Report the Issue to the Service Provider** – Most platforms have a recovery process to help users reclaim hacked accounts.

How to Recover a Stolen Identity or Financial Losses

Understanding Identity Theft

Identity theft occurs when someone uses your personal information—such as your Social Security number, bank details, or credit card information—without your permission. This can lead to financial fraud, unauthorized transactions, or even legal issues.

Steps to Take if Your Identity is Stolen

- **Contact Your Bank and Credit Card Providers** – Report unauthorized transactions and request a fraud alert on your accounts.
- **Change Passwords and Secure Your Accounts** – Update login credentials for banking, email, and other sensitive accounts.
- **Monitor Your Credit Reports** – Regularly review your credit reports for unfamiliar activities.
- **Report the Theft to Authorities** – File a report with law enforcement and cybersecurity agencies to document the fraud.
- **Freeze or Lock Your Credit** – Prevent further damage by restricting access to your credit report.

Reporting Cybercrimes and Scams

When and Why to Report Cybercrimes

Reporting cybercrimes helps authorities track criminal activity and prevent further harm. Common reportable offenses include:

- Phishing scams
- Financial fraud
- Online harassment or blackmail
- Unauthorized access to personal accounts

How to File a Report

- **Document the Evidence** – Keep screenshots, emails, and transaction records.
- **Contact Law Enforcement** – File a report with local authorities or cybersecurity agencies.
- **Report to Online Platforms** – Inform social media networks, email providers, or e-commerce platforms where the scam occurred.
- **Alert Your Bank or Financial Institution** – If financial fraud is involved, notify your bank immediately.

Staying Proactive: Creating a Long-Term Cybersecurity Plan

Establishing Good Cybersecurity Habits

To prevent future cybersecurity threats, adopt these best practices:

- Use strong, unique passwords for each account
- Enable two-factor authentication wherever possible
- Keep your software and devices updated
- Regularly review account activity
- Stay informed about emerging threats

Regular Cybersecurity Maintenance

- **Perform routine security scans** – Schedule weekly antivirus and malware scans.
- **Monitor your financial and online accounts** – Check bank statements and email logs frequently.
- **Backup your important data** – Store backups offline or in a secure cloud service.
- **Educate family members** – Make sure everyone in your household follows security best practices.

By implementing these strategies, you can significantly reduce the risk of cyber threats and stay one step ahead of potential attackers.

Conclusion: Becoming a Cyber-Smart User

Cybersecurity is not just a technical subject reserved for IT professionals—it is a necessary skill for everyone who uses the internet. Throughout this guide, you have learned about various online threats, best practices for securing your accounts, and how to develop a strong digital defense. But learning about cybersecurity is not a one-time event; it is an ongoing process that requires awareness, vigilance, and consistent effort.

The digital world is evolving rapidly, and cybercriminals are becoming more sophisticated in their attack methods. This means you must stay proactive in protecting yourself, your devices, and your personal information. A cyber-smart user is not someone who never encounters threats but rather someone who knows how to recognize risks and respond effectively. The more you practice safe habits, the more second nature they will become.

By applying the knowledge in this book, you are taking an essential step toward a safer online experience. As we wrap up, let's go over the key takeaways, explore what the future of cybersecurity holds, and reinforce final tips to ensure you remain protected every day.

Key Takeaways from This Guide

Here is a summary of the most important lessons you have learned in this guide:

1. Understanding Cyber Threats

- Cyber threats come in many forms, including malware, phishing, identity theft, and online scams.
- Hackers exploit vulnerabilities in weak passwords, outdated software, and unsecure networks to gain access to personal and financial data.

2. Creating Strong Passwords and Securing Accounts

- Weak passwords make it easy for cybercriminals to break into accounts.
- Always use strong, unique passwords for each account and store them in a trusted password manager.
- Enabling Two-Factor Authentication (2FA) adds an extra layer of security to prevent unauthorized access.

3. Protecting Your Devices and Home Network

- Keeping your devices updated ensures they have the latest security patches.
- Firewalls, antivirus programs, and secure Wi-Fi settings help safeguard your devices from intrusions.
- Avoid using public Wi-Fi without a Virtual Private Network (VPN) to protect your data from being intercepted.

4. Safe Browsing and Email Security

- Always check website URLs for "https" to ensure they are secure before entering personal information.
- Phishing emails often trick users into clicking malicious links or downloading harmful files—verify the sender before interacting.
- Be cautious of pop-ups, fake ads, and suspicious attachments.

5. Social Media and Online Privacy

- Oversharing personal details online increases the risk of identity theft and fraud.
- Adjust your privacy settings on social media platforms to control who sees your information.
- Be wary of friend requests or messages from strangers who may have malicious intentions.

6. Online Shopping and Banking Security

- Use secure payment methods like PayPal or virtual credit cards to protect financial transactions.
- Be cautious of fake e-commerce websites and never enter payment details on unfamiliar platforms.
- Monitor your bank accounts for unauthorized transactions and report any suspicious activity immediately.

7. Protecting Children and Families Online

- Educating children about online safety helps them develop good digital habits.
- Parental controls can help restrict access to inappropriate websites and monitor screen time.

- Teach kids how to recognize cyberbullying and scams, and encourage open communication about their online experiences.

The Future of Cybersecurity and Emerging Threats

While we have covered many current threats and best practices, cybersecurity is a constantly evolving field. As technology advances, so do the methods that cybercriminals use to exploit users. Here are some key trends and emerging threats you should be aware of:

1. AI-Powered Cyber Attacks

Artificial Intelligence (AI) is being used not only for security but also by hackers to automate attacks, create sophisticated phishing emails, and bypass security measures. AI-powered malware can quickly adapt and spread faster than traditional viruses.

2. Internet of Things (IoT) Security Risks

As smart home devices like security cameras, smart thermostats, and voice assistants become more common, they introduce new vulnerabilities. Many IoT devices have weak security, making them prime targets for hackers to exploit.

3. Deepfake Scams and Fraud

Deepfake technology can create convincing fake videos and voices, making it harder to distinguish between real and manipulated content. This can be used for identity theft, financial fraud, and spreading misinformation.

4. Ransomware on the Rise

Ransomware attacks, where hackers encrypt a user's files and demand payment for their release, are increasing. These attacks now target individuals, businesses, and even government institutions.

5. The Expansion of the Dark Web

Cybercriminals use the dark web to buy and sell stolen data, hacking tools, and illegal services. Awareness of how stolen credentials are used can help individuals take extra precautions with their data.

Staying informed about these threats is just as important as practicing cybersecurity habits. Keeping up with security news, enabling automatic updates, and using advanced protective measures will help you stay one step ahead.

Final Tips for Staying Safe Online Every Day

To maintain a strong defense against cyber threats, incorporate these daily habits into your routine:

1. Stay Cautious and Think Before You Click

- If an email, message, or link looks suspicious, verify its authenticity before clicking.
- Avoid downloading attachments from unknown sources.

2. Regularly Update and Maintain Your Devices

- Enable automatic updates for your operating system, apps, and antivirus software.
- Remove unused apps and accounts to minimize security risks.

3. Use Secure Connections at All Times

- Always use a VPN when connecting to public Wi-Fi.
- Lock your devices with strong passwords or biometric authentication (fingerprint, face recognition).

4. Be Mindful of Your Online Presence

- Limit the amount of personal information you share on social media.
- Regularly review and adjust your privacy settings.

5. Backup Important Data Regularly

- Keep backups of important files on an external drive or cloud storage.
- Set up automatic backups to prevent data loss in case of an attack.

6. Educate Yourself and Others

- Cybersecurity awareness is an ongoing process—stay informed about new threats.
- Teach family members and friends about safe online practices.

7. Monitor Your Financial Accounts for Unusual Activity

- Set up alerts for banking transactions.
- Immediately report unauthorized transactions to your bank.

Final Thoughts

Cybersecurity is not about achieving 100% safety—it's about reducing risks and making yourself a less likely target for cybercriminals. The more security measures you apply, the more difficult it becomes for hackers to breach your accounts or steal your information.

By implementing the strategies discussed in this book, you can navigate the digital world with confidence, knowing that you are taking the right steps to protect yourself. Keep learning, stay updated on cybersecurity trends, and make security a habit rather than an afterthought.

Remember, your online safety is in your hands—be smart, be cautious, and always stay one step ahead of cyber threats!

Appendices

1. Cybersecurity Terms Glossary – Definitions of Common Cybersecurity Terms

Understanding cybersecurity begins with knowing the key terms used in the field. Whether you are a beginner or someone looking to strengthen your knowledge, this glossary will help you understand critical cybersecurity concepts in simple terms. Each term is explained in an easy-to-understand way, making it accessible for readers of all levels.

Common Cybersecurity Terms and Their Definitions

- **Antivirus** – A program designed to detect, prevent, and remove malicious software (malware) from a computer or device.
- **Authentication** – The process of verifying the identity of a user, device, or system before granting access.
- **Backup** – A copy of important data stored separately to protect against loss or corruption.
- **Botnet** – A network of infected computers controlled remotely by cybercriminals to carry out attacks.
- **Brute Force Attack** – A hacking method that uses automated tools to guess passwords by trying numerous combinations.
- **Data Breach** – An incident where sensitive, protected, or confidential data is accessed or stolen by unauthorized individuals.

- **Encryption** – A method of converting data into a coded format to prevent unauthorized access.
- **Firewall** – A security system that monitors and controls incoming and outgoing network traffic to block malicious activity.
- **Malware** – Any software designed to harm, exploit, or disable devices, networks, or services. Includes viruses, worms, ransomware, and spyware.
- **Phishing** – A deceptive attempt to steal sensitive information by pretending to be a trustworthy source, often through emails or fake websites.
- **Ransomware** – A type of malware that locks or encrypts a victim's files and demands payment to restore access.
- **Spyware** – Malicious software that secretly collects user information without their knowledge.
- **Two-Factor Authentication (2FA)** – An extra security layer that requires two forms of verification (e.g., password and mobile code) to log into an account.
- **Zero-Day Attack** – An attack that exploits a software vulnerability before the developer has released a fix.

This is just a selection of common terms. The more familiar you become with cybersecurity language, the better equipped you'll be to protect yourself online.

2. Cybersecurity Tools and Software Recommendations – Best Free and Paid Security Tools

Keeping your devices and online accounts secure requires the right set of tools. Cybersecurity software helps protect against malware, phishing, identity theft, and other online threats. Below is a list of some of the best free and paid security tools for different areas of protection.

Antivirus and Anti-Malware Software

Having a reliable antivirus program is essential for detecting and removing malicious threats.

Free Options:

- **Windows Defender** (Built-in for Windows) – Provides real-time protection against malware.
- **Avast Free Antivirus** – Offers good basic protection against viruses and malware.
- **Malwarebytes Free** – Great for scanning and removing existing malware infections.

Paid Options:

- **Norton 360** – Provides full antivirus protection with additional features like VPN and dark web monitoring.
- **Bitdefender Total Security** – Offers advanced protection against malware, ransomware, and phishing.
- **Malwarebytes Premium** – A stronger version of the free Malwarebytes with real-time protection.

Password Managers

Managing passwords securely is crucial for online safety.

Free Options:

- **Bitwarden** – An open-source, secure password manager.
- **LastPass (Free Plan)** – Stores and auto-fills passwords securely.

Paid Options:

- **1Password** – Offers advanced encryption and password-sharing features.
- **Dashlane Premium** – Provides password storage, auto-login, and dark web monitoring.

Virtual Private Networks (VPNs)

VPNs help secure your online activity by encrypting internet traffic.

Free Options:

- **ProtonVPN (Free Plan)** – No data limits, good for privacy protection.
- **Windscribe Free** – Provides limited data but good encryption.

Paid Options:

- **NordVPN** – One of the most secure VPNs with high-speed connections.
- **ExpressVPN** – Offers strong encryption and works well with streaming services.

- **CyberGhost VPN** – Great for anonymous browsing and secure streaming.

Firewall Protection

A firewall monitors incoming and outgoing network traffic to block malicious activity.

- **Windows and macOS Built-in Firewalls** – Free and effective for most users.
- **GlassWire (Paid)** – Offers advanced network monitoring and security alerts.

Secure Browsing Extensions

Enhance your web security with browser extensions.

- **HTTPS Everywhere** (Free) – Forces websites to use secure HTTPS connections.
- **uBlock Origin** (Free) – Blocks ads and malicious scripts.
- **Privacy Badger** (Free) – Stops websites from tracking your online activity.

Using a combination of these tools can significantly improve your cybersecurity posture and keep your data safe.

---

3. Emergency Cybersecurity Response Checklist – Quick Actions to Take During a Cyberattack

Cyberattacks can happen unexpectedly, and quick action can help minimize damage. Use this checklist as an emergency guide if you experience a cybersecurity incident.

Step 1: Identify the Threat

- Check for unusual activity (slow performance, unexpected pop-ups, unauthorized account logins, etc.).
- Look for suspicious emails, messages, or links that may have triggered the issue.

Step 2: Disconnect Affected Devices

- Immediately disconnect from Wi-Fi or unplug the Ethernet cable to stop malware from spreading.
- Turn off Bluetooth and any external storage devices.

Step 3: Run a Security Scan

- Use your antivirus or anti-malware software to scan for threats.
- If your computer is heavily compromised, boot into Safe Mode and run the scan again.

Step 4: Change Important Passwords

- Use a secure device to change passwords for critical accounts (email, banking, social media).
- Enable Two-Factor Authentication (2FA) wherever possible.

Step 5: Secure Your Accounts and Devices

- Log out from all devices and reset active sessions.
- Remove unauthorized devices from your accounts.
- Update your operating system and security software.

Step 6: Report the Incident

- If it's a financial fraud or identity theft, contact your bank and freeze your accounts if necessary.
- Report phishing emails to your email provider.
- If your data was exposed in a breach, monitor your credit report and online accounts.

Step 7: Prevent Future Attacks

- Enable automatic updates for your operating system and software.
- Regularly back up your files to an external hard drive or cloud storage.
- Educate yourself and others on safe online practices.

Following this checklist can help you respond quickly and effectively during a cybersecurity incident, minimizing risks and protecting your information.

www.ingramcontent.com/pod-product-compliance
Lightning Source LLC
LaVergne TN
LVHW052056060326
832903LV00061B/990